Understanding JavaScript Promises

Nicholas C. Zakas

Understanding JavaScript Promises

Nicholas C. Zakas

ISBN 978-1-6780-3415-3

Copyright 2020-2022 Nicholas C. Zakas. All rights reserved.

Contents

Introduction 5
   About This Book 5
   Acknowledgments 8
   About the Author 8
   Disclaimer 8

1. Promise Basics 9
   The Promise Lifecycle 9
   Creating New (Unsettled) Promises 17
   Creating Settled Promises 20
   Summary 23

2. Chaining Promises 25
   Catching Errors 26
   Using finally() in Promise Chains 28
   Returning Values in Promise Chains 31
   Returning Promises in Promise Chains 33
   Summary 39

3. Working with Multiple Promises 41
   The Promise.all() Method 41
   The Promise.allSettled() Method 48
   The Promise.any() Method 54
   The Promise.race() Method 58
   Summary 61

4. Async Functions and Await Expressions 63
Defining Async Functions 63
What Makes Async Functions Different 65
Summary 77

5. Unhandled Rejection Tracking 79
Detecting Unhandled Rejections 79
Web Browser Unhandled Rejection Tracking 81
Node.js Unhandled Rejection Tracking 85
Summary 88

Final Thoughts 91
Download the Extras 91
Support the Author 91
Help and Support 92
Follow the Author 92

Introduction

One of the most powerful aspects of JavaScript is how easily it handles asynchronous programming. As a language created for the web, JavaScript needed to respond to user interactions such as clicks and key presses from the beginning, and so event handlers such as `onclick` were created. Event handlers allowed developers to specify a function to execute at some later point in time in reaction to an event.

Node.js further popularized asynchronous programming in JavaScript by using callback functions in addition to events. As more and more programs started using asynchronous programming, events and callbacks were no longer sufficient to support everything developers wanted to do. *Promises* are the solution to this problem.

Promises are another option for asynchronous programming, and they work like futures and deferreds do in other languages. A promise specifies some code to be executed later (as with events and callbacks) and also explicitly indicates whether the code succeeded or failed at its job. You can chain promises together based on success or failure in ways that make your code easier to understand and debug.

About This Book

The goal of this book is to explain how JavaScript promises work while giving practical examples of when to use them. All new asynchronous JavaScript APIs will be built with promises going forward, and so promises are a central concept to understanding JavaScript as a whole. My hope is that this book will give you the information you need to successfully use promises in your projects.

Browser, Node.js, and Deno Compatibility

There are multiple JavaScript runtimes that you may use, such as web browsers, Node.js, and Deno. This book doesn't attempt to address differences between these JavaScript runtimes unless they are so different as to be confusing. In general, this book focuses on promises as described in ECMA-262 and only talks about differences in JavaScript runtimes when they are substantially different. As such, it's possible that your JavaScript runtime may not conform to the standards-based behavior described in this book.

Who This Book Is for

This book is intended as a guide for those who are already familiar with JavaScript. In particular, this book is aimed at intermediate-to-advanced JavaScript developers who work in web browsers, Node.js, or Deno and who want to learn how promises work.

This book is not for beginners who have never written JavaScript. You will need to have a good, basic understanding of the language to make use of this book.

Overview

Each of this book's five chapters covers a different aspect of JavaScript promises. Many chapters cover promise APIs directly, and each chapter builds upon the preceding chapters in a way that allows you to build up your knowledge gradually. All chapters include code examples to help you learn new syntax and concepts.

Chapter 1: Promise Basics introduces the concept of promises, how they work, and different ways to create and use them.

Chapter 2: Chaining Promises discusses the various ways to chain multiple promises together to make composing asynchronous operations easier.

Chapter 3: Working with Multiple Promises explains the built-in JavaScript methods designed to monitor and respond to multiple promises executing in parallel.

Chapter 4: Async Functions and Await Expressions introduces the concepts of async functions and `await` expressions, and explains how they relate to and use promises.

Chapter 5: Unhandled Rejection Tracking explains how to properly track when promises are rejected without a rejection handler.

Conventions Used

The following typographical conventions are used in this book:

- *Italics* introduces new terms
- `Constant width` indicates a piece of code or filename

All JavaScript code examples are written as modules (also known as ECMAScript modules or ESM).

Additionally, longer code examples are contained in constant width code blocks such as:

```
function doSomething() {
    // empty
}
```

Within a code block, comments to the right of a `console.log()` statement indicate the output you'll see in the browser or Node.js console when the code is executed. For example:

```
console.log("Hi");      // "Hi"
```

If a line of code in a code block throws an error, this is also indicated to the right of the code:

```
doSomething();          // error!
```

Help and Support

If you have questions as you read this book, please send a message to my mailing list: books@humanwhocodes.com. Be sure to mention the title of this book in your subject line.

Acknowledgments

I'm grateful to my father, Speros Zakas, for copyediting this book and for Rob Friesel's technical editing. You both have made this book much better than it was.

Thanks to everyone who reviewed early versions of this book and provided feedback: Mike Sherov, David Hund, Murat Corlu, and Chris Ferdinandi.

About the Author

Nicholas C. Zakas is an independent software engineer, consultant, and coach. He is the creator of the ESLint open source project and serves on the ESLint Technical Steering Committee. Nicholas works with companies and individuals to improve software engineering processes and helps technical leaders grow and succeed. He has also authored or contributed to over a dozen books related to JavaScript and web development. You can find Nicholas online at humanwhocodes.com and on Twitter @slicknet.

Disclaimer

While the publisher and the author have used good faith effort to ensure that the information and instructions contained in this work are accurate, the publisher and the author disclaim all responsibility for errors or omissions, including without limitation responsibility for damages resulting from the use of or reliance on this work. Use of the information and instructions contained in this work is at your own risk. If any code samples or other technology this work contains or describes is subject to open source licenses or the intellectual property rights of others, it is your responsibility to ensure that your use thereof complies with such licenses and/or rights.

1. Promise Basics

While promises are often associated with asynchronous operations, they are simply placeholders for values. The value may already be known or, more commonly, the value may be the result of an asynchronous operation. Instead of subscribing to an event or passing a callback to a function, a function can return a promise, like this:

```
// fetch() promises to complete at some point in the future
const promise = fetch("books.json");
```

The `fetch()` function is a common utility function in JavaScript runtimes that makes network requests. The call to `fetch()` doesn't actually complete a network request immediately; that will happen later. Instead, the function returns a promise object (stored in the `promise` variable in this example, but you can name it whatever you want) representing the asynchronous operation so you can work with it in the future. Exactly when you'll be able to work with that result depends entirely on how the promise's lifecycle plays out.

The Promise Lifecycle

Each promise goes through a short lifecycle starting in the *pending* state, which indicates that promise hasn't completed yet. A pending promise is considered *unsettled*. The promise in the previous example is in the pending state as soon as the `fetch()` function returns it. Once the promise completes, the promise is considered *settled* and enters one of two possible states (see Figure 1-1):

1. *Fulfilled*: The promise has completed successfully.
2. *Rejected*: The promise didn't complete successfully due to either an error or some other cause.

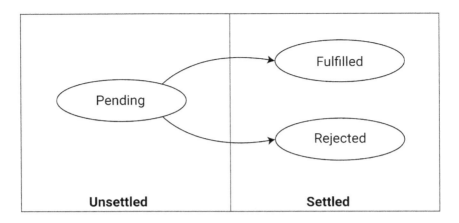

Figure 1-1: Promise states

An internal [[PromiseState]] property is set to "pending", "fulfilled", or "rejected" to reflect the promise's state. This property isn't exposed on promise objects, so you can't determine which state the promise is in programmatically. But you can take a specific action when a promise changes state by using the then() method.

Assigning Handlers with then()

The then() method is present on all promises and takes two arguments. The first argument is a function to call when the promise is fulfilled, called the *fulfillment handler*. Any additional data related to the asynchronous operation is passed to this function. The second argument is a function to call when the promise is rejected, called the *rejection handler*. Similar to the fulfillment handler, the rejection handler is passed any additional data related to the rejection.

> Any object that implements the then() method in this way is called a *thenable*. All promises are thenables, but not all thenables are promises.

Both arguments to then() are optional, so you can listen for any combination of fulfillment and rejection. For example, consider this set of then() calls:

```
const promise = fetch("books.json");

// add a fulfillment and rejection handler
promise.then(response => {
    // fulfillment
    console.log(response.status);
}, reason => {
    // rejection
    console.error(reason.message);
});

// add another fulfillment handler
promise.then(response => {
    // fulfillment
    console.log(response.statusText);
});

// add another rejection handler
promise.then(null, reason => {
    // rejection
    console.error(reason.message);
});
```

All three then() calls operate on the same promise. The first call assigns both a fulfillment and a rejection handler. The second only assigns a fulfillment handler; errors won't be reported. The third just assigns a rejection handler and doesn't report success.

One quirk of the `fetch()` function is that the returned promise is fulfilled whenever it receives an HTTP status, even 404 or 500. The promise is only rejected when the network request fails for some reason. If you want to ensure that the status is in the 200-299 range, you can check the `response.ok` property, as in this example:

```
const promise = fetch("books.json");

promise.then(response => {
    if (response.ok) {
        console.log("Request succeeded.");
    } else {
        console.error("Request failed.");
    }
});
```

Assigning Rejection Handlers with `catch()`

Promises also have a `catch()` method that behaves the same as `then()` when only a rejection handler is passed. For example, the following `catch()` and `then()` calls are functionally equivalent:

```
const promise = fetch("books.json");

promise.catch(reason => {
    // rejection
    console.error(reason.message);
});

// is the same as:

promise.then(null, reason => {
    // rejection
    console.error(reason.message);
});
```

The intent behind `then()` and `catch()` is for you to use them in combination to clearly indicate how a result is handled. This system is better than events and callbacks because it makes success or failure completely clear. (Events tend not to fire when there's an error, and in callbacks you must always remember to check the error argument.) Just know that if you don't attach a rejection handler to a promise that is rejected, then the JavaScript runtime will output a message to the console, or throw an error, or both (depending on the runtime).

Assigning Settlement Handlers with `finally()`

To go along with `then()` and `catch()` there is also `finally()`. The callback passed to `finally()` (called a *settlement handler*) is called regardless of success or failure. Unlike the callbacks for `then()` and `catch()`, `finally()` callbacks do not receive any arguments because it isn't clear whether the promise was fulfilled or rejected. Because the settlement handler is called both on fulfillment and rejection, it is similar (but not the same; discussed further in Chapter 2) to passing the handler for both fulfillment and rejection using `then()`. Here's an example:

```
const promise = fetch("books.json");

promise.finally(() => {
    // no way to know if fulfilled or rejected
    console.log("Settled");
});

// is similar to:

const callback = () => {
    console.log("Settled");
};

promise.then(callback, callback);
```

As long as you don't access the argument passed to `callback`, the behavior between these two examples is the same. However, as with `catch()`, using `finally()` makes your intention clearer as compared to `then()`.

Settlement handlers are useful when you want to know that an operation has completed and you don't care about the result. As an example, you may want to display a loading indicator on a web page while a `fetch()` request is active and then hide it when the request is complete. It doesn't matter if the request was successful or not because the loading indicator should stop once the request is complete. You might have code like this in your web application:

```
const appElement = document.getElementById("app");
const promise = fetch("books.json");

appElement.classList.add("loading");

promise.then(() => {
    // handle success
});

promise.catch(() => {
    // handle failure
});

promise.finally(() => {
    appElement.classList.remove("loading");
});
```

Here, `appElement` represents the HTML element that wraps the entire application on the page. A network request is initiated using `fetch()` and the CSS class `"loading"` is added to the HTML element (allowing you to change any styles as appropriate). When the network request completes, `promise` is settled and the settlement handler removes the `"loading"` class from the HTML element to reset the application state. You can still respond to success and failure using `then()` and `catch()` while `finally()` solely handles the state change. Without `finally()`, you would need to remove the `"loading"` class in both the fulfillment and rejection handlers.

> The settlement handlers added with `finally()` do not prevent rejections from outputting an error to the console or throwing an error. You must still add a rejection handler to prevent the error from being thrown in that case.

Assigning Handlers to Settled Promises

A fulfillment, rejection, or settlement handler will still be executed even if it is added after the promise is already settled. This allows you to add new fulfillment and rejection handlers at any time and guarantee that they will be called. For example:

```
const promise = fetch("books.json");

// original fulfillment handler
promise.then(response => {
    console.log(response.status);

    // now add another
    promise.then(response => {
        console.log(response.statusText);
    });
});
```

In this code, the fulfillment handler adds another fulfillment handler to the same promise. The promise is already fulfilled at this point, so the new fulfillment handler is added to the microtask queue and called when ready. Rejection and settlement handlers work the same way.

Handlers and Microtasks

JavaScript executed in the regular flow of a program is executed as a *task*, which is to say that the JavaScript runtime has created a new execution context and executes the code completely, exiting when finished. As an example, an `onclick` handler for a button in a web page is executed as a task. When the button is clicked, a new task is created and the `onclick` handler is executed. Once complete, the JavaScript runtime waits for the next interaction to execute more code. Promise handlers, however, are executed in a different way.

All promise handlers, whether fulfillment, rejection, or settlement, are executed as *microtasks* inside of the JavaScript engine. Microtasks are queued and then executed immediately after the currently running task has completed, before the JavaScript runtime becomes idle. Calling `then()`, `catch()`, or `finally()` tells a promise to queue the specified microtasks once the promise is settled.

This is different than creating timers using `setTimeout()` or `setInterval()`, both of which create new tasks to be executed at a later point in time. Queued promise handlers will always execute before timers that are queued in the same task. You can test this for yourself by using the global `queueMicrotask()` function, which is used to create microtasks outside of promises:

```
setTimeout(() => {
    console.log("timer");

    queueMicrotask(() => {
        console.log("microtask in timer");
    });

}, 0);

queueMicrotask(() => {
    console.log("microtask");
});
```

In this code, a timer is created with a delay of 0 milliseconds, and inside of that timer a new microtask is created. Also, a microtask is created outside of the timer. When this code executes, you will see the following output to the console:

```
microtask
timer
microtask in timer
```

Even though the timer is set for a delay of 0 milliseconds, the microtask executes first, followed by the timer, followed by the microtask inside of the timer.

The most important thing to remember about microtasks, including all promise handlers, is that they are executed as soon as possible once a task is complete. This minimizes the amount of time between a promise settling and the reaction to the settling, making promises suitable for situations where runtime performance is important.

Creating New (Unsettled) Promises

New promises are created using the `Promise` constructor. This constructor accepts a single argument: a function called the *executor*, which contains the code to initialize the promise. The executor is passed two functions named `resolve()` and `reject()` as arguments. You call the `resolve()` function when the executor has finished successfully to signal that the promise is resolved or the `reject()` function to indicate that the operation has failed.

Here's an example using the old `XMLHttpRequest` browser API:

```
// Browser example

function requestURL(url) {
    return new Promise((resolve, reject) => {

        const xhr = new XMLHttpRequest();

        // assign event handlers
        xhr.addEventListener("load", () => {
            resolve({
                status: xhr.status,
                text: xhr.responseText
            });
        });

        xhr.addEventListener("error", error => {
            reject(error);
        });

        // send the request
        xhr.open("get", url);
        xhr.send();
    });
}

const promise = requestURL("books.json");
```

```
// listen for both fulfillment and rejection
promise.then(response => {
    // fulfillment
    console.log(response.status);
    console.log(response.text);
}, reason => {
    // rejection
    console.error(reason.message);
});
```

In this example, the `XMLHttpRequest` call is wrapped in a promise. The `load` event indicates when a request has completed successfully, and so the promise executor calls `resolve()` in the event handler. Similarly, the `error` event indicates when the request couldn't be completed and so `reject()` is called in that event handler. You can follow this same process (using `resolve()` and `reject()` in event handlers) for converting event-based functionality into promise-based functionality.

One important aspect of executors is that they run immediately upon creation of the promise. In the previous example, the `xhr` object is created, event handlers assigned, and the call initiated before the promise is returned from `requestURL()`. When either `resolve()` or `reject()` is called inside the executor, then the promise's state and value are immediately set, but all promise handlers (being microtasks) will not execute until the current script job completes. For example, consider what happens if you call `resolve()` immediately inside an executor, as in this code:

```
const promise = new Promise((resolve, reject) => {
    console.log("Executor");
    resolve(42);
});

promise.then(result => {
    console.log(result);
});

console.log("Hi!");
```

Here, the promise is resolved immediately without any delay, and then a fulfillment handler is added using `then()` to output the result. Even though the promise is already resolved when the fulfillment handler is added, the output will be as follows:

```
Executor
Hi!
42
```

The executor is run first, outputting "Executor" to the console. Next, the fulfillment handler is assigned but is not executed immediately. Instead, a new microtask is created to run after the current script job. That means console.log("Hi!") executes before the fulfillment handler, which outputs 42 after the rest of the script has completed.

> A promise can only be resolved once, so if you call resolve() more than once inside of an executor, every call after the first is ignored.

Executor Errors

If an error is thrown inside an executor, then the promise's rejection handler is called. For example:

```
const promise = new Promise((resolve, reject) => {
    throw new Error("Uh oh!");
});

promise.catch(reason => {
    console.log(reason.message);     // "Uh oh!"
});
```

In this code, the executor intentionally throws an error. There is an implicit try-catch inside every executor so that the error is caught and then passed to the rejection handler. The previous example is equivalent to:

```
const promise = new Promise((resolve, reject) => {
    try {
        throw new Error("Uh oh!");
    } catch (ex) {
        reject(ex);
    }
});

promise.catch(reason => {
    console.log(reason.message);     // "Uh oh!"
});
```

The executor handles catching any thrown errors to simplify this common use case, and just like other rejections, the JavaScript engine throws an error and stops execution if no rejection handler is assigned.

Creating Settled Promises

The `Promise` constructor is the best way to create unsettled promises due to the dynamic nature of what the promise executor does. But if you want a promise to represent a previously computed value, then it doesn't make sense to create an executor that simply passes a value to the `resolve()` or `reject()` function. Instead, there are two methods that create settled promises given a specific value.

> Creating settled promises is helpful for compatibility with APIs that expect promises to be passed as arguments.

Using Promise.resolve()

The `Promise.resolve()` method accepts a single argument and returns a promise in the fulfilled state. That means you don't have to supply an executor if you know the value of the promise already. For example:

```
const promise = Promise.resolve(42);

promise.then(value => {
    console.log(value);         // 42
});
```

This code creates a fulfilled promise so the fulfillment handler receives 42 as `value`. As with other examples in this chapter, the fulfillment handler is executed as a microtask after the current script job completes. If a rejection handler were added to this promise, the rejection handler would never be called because the promise will never be in the rejected state.

> If you pass a promise to `Promise.resolve()`, then the function returns the same promise that you passed in. For example:
>
> ```
> const promise1 = Promise.resolve(42);
> const promise2 = Promise.resolve(promise1);
>
> console.log(promise1 === promise2);          // true
> ```

Using Promise.reject()

You can also create rejected promises by using the `Promise.reject()` method. This works like `Promise.resolve()` except the created promise is in the rejected state, as follows:

```
const promise = Promise.reject(42);

promise.catch(reason => {
    console.log(reason);        // 42
});
```

Any additional rejection handlers added to this promise would be called, but fulfillment handlers will not because the promise will never be in the fulfilled state.

> If you pass a promise to either the `Promise.resolve()` or `Promise.reject()` methods, the promise is returned without modification.

Non-Promise Thenables

Both `Promise.resolve()` and `Promise.reject()` also accept non-promise thenables as arguments. When passed a non-promise thenable, these methods create a new promise that is settled with the same value and state of the settled thenable.

A non-promise thenable is created when an object has a `then()` method that accepts a `resolve` and a `reject` argument, like this:

```
const thenable = {
    then(resolve, reject) {
        resolve(42);
    }
};
```

The `thenable` object in this example has no characteristics associated with a promise other than the `then()` method. You can call `Promise.resolve()` to convert `thenable` into a fulfilled promise:

```
const thenable = {
    then(resolve, reject) {
        resolve(42);
    }
};

const promise = Promise.resolve(thenable);
promise.then(value => {
    console.log(value);     // 42
});
```

In this example, `Promise.resolve()` calls `thenable.then()` so that a promise state can be determined. The promise state for `thenable` is fulfilled because `resolve(42)` is called inside the `then()` method. A new promise called `promise` is created in the fulfilled state with the value passed from `thenable` (that is, 42), and the fulfillment handler for `promise` receives 42 as the value.

The same process can be used with `Promise.resolve()` to create a rejected promise from a thenable:

```
const thenable = {
    then(resolve, reject) {
        reject(42);
    }
};

const promise = Promise.resolve(thenable);
promise.catch(value => {
    console.log(value);     // 42
});
```

This example is similar to the last except that thenable is rejected. When thenable.then() executes, a new promise is created in the rejected state with a value of 42. That value is then passed to the rejection handler for promise.

Promise.resolve() and Promise.reject() work like this to allow you to easily work with non-promise thenables. A lot of libraries used thenables prior to promises being introduced in 2015, so the ability to convert thenables into formal promises is important for backwards compatibility with previously existing libraries. When you're unsure if an object is a promise, passing the object through Promise.resolve() or Promise.reject() (depending on your anticipated result) is the best way to find out because promises just pass through unchanged.

Summary

A promise is a placeholder for a value that may be provided later as the result of some asynchronous operation. Instead of assigning an event handler or passing a callback into a function, you can use a promise to represent the result of an operation.

Promises have three states: pending, fulfilled, and rejected. A promise starts in a pending (unsettled) state and becomes fulfilled on a successful execution or rejected on a failure (fulfillment and rejection are settled states). In either case, handlers can be added to indicate when a promise is settled. The then() method allows you to assign a fulfillment and rejection handler; the catch() method allows you to assign only a rejection handler; the finally() method allows you to assign a settlement handler that is always called regardless of the outcome. All promise handlers are run as microtasks so they will not execute until the current script job is complete.

You can create new unsettled promises using the `Promise` constructor, which accepts an executor function as its only argument. The executor function is passed `resolve()` and `reject()` functions that you use to indicate the success or failure of the promise. The executor runs immediately upon creation of the promise, unlike handlers, which are run as microtasks. Any errors thrown in an executor are automatically caught and passed to `reject()`.

It's possible to create settled promises using `Promise.resolve()` for fulfilled promises and `Promise.reject()` for rejected promises. Each method will wrap its argument in a promise (if it's not a promise and not a non-promise thenable), create a new promise (for non-promise thenables), or pass through any existing promise. These methods are helpful when you are unsure if the value is a promise but want it to behave like one.

While creating single promises is a useful and effective way to work with asynchronous operations in JavaScript, promises allow interesting composition patterns when chained together. In the next chapter, you'll learn how promise handlers work to create promise chains and why that's a valuable capability.

2. Chaining Promises

To this point, promises may seem like little more than an incremental improvement over using some combination of a callback and the `setTimeout()` function, but there is much more to promises than meets the eye. More specifically, there are a number of ways to chain promises together to accomplish more complex asynchronous behavior.

Each call to `then()`, `catch()`, or `finally()` actually creates and returns another promise. This second promise is settled only once the first has been fulfilled or rejected. Consider this example:

```
const promise = Promise.resolve(42);

promise.then(value => {
    console.log(value);
}).then(() => {
    console.log("Finished");
});
```

The code outputs:

```
42
Finished
```

The call to `promise.then()` returns a second promise on which `then()` is called. The second `then()` fulfillment handler is only called after the first promise has been resolved. If you unchain this example, it looks like this:

```
const promise1 = Promise.resolve(42);

const promise2 = promise1.then(value => {
    console.log(value);
});

promise2.then(() => {
    console.log("Finished");
});
```

In this unchained version of the code, the result of `promise1.then()` is stored in `promise2`, and then `promise2.then()` is called to add the final fulfillment handler. The call to `promise2.then()` also returns a promise. This example just doesn't use that promise.

Catching Errors

Promise chaining allows you to catch errors that may occur in a fulfillment or rejection handler from a previous promise. For example:

```
const promise = Promise.resolve(42);

promise.then(value => {
    throw new Error("Oops!");
}).catch(reason => {
    console.error(reason.message);     // "Oops!"
});
```

In this code, the fulfillment handler for `promise` throws an error. The chained call to the `catch()` method, which is on a second promise, is able to receive that error through its rejection handler. The same is true if a rejection handler throws an error:

```
const promise = new Promise((resolve, reject) => {
    throw new Error("Uh oh!");
});
```

```
promise.catch(reason => {
    console.log(reason.message);    // "Uh oh!"
    throw new Error("Oops!");
}).catch(reason => {
    console.error(reason.message);  // "Oops!"
});
```

Here, the executor throws an error that triggers the `promise`'s rejection handler. That handler then throws another error that is caught by the second promise's rejection handler. The chained promise calls are aware of errors in other promises in the chain.

You can use this ability to catch errors through a promise chain to effectively act like a `try-catch` statement. Consider using `fetch()` to retrieve some data and wanting to catch any errors that occur:

```
const promise = fetch("books.json");

promise.then(response => {
    console.log(response.status);
}).catch(reason => {
    console.error(reason.message);
});
```

This example will output the response status from the `fetch()` call if it succeeds and will output the error message if the call fails. You can take this a step further and handle status codes outside of the 200-299 range as errors by checking the `response.ok` property (discussed in Chapter 1) and throwing an error if it is `false`, as in this example:

```
const promise = fetch("books.json");

promise.then(response => {
    if (response.ok) {
        console.log(response.status);
    } else {
        throw new Error(`Unexpected status code: ${
            response.status
        } ${response.statusText}`);
```

```
        }
    }).catch(reason => {
        console.error(reason.message);
    });
```

The chained `catch()` call in this example creates a rejection handler that catches both errors returned by `fetch()` and also any errors thrown in the fulfillment handler. So instead of needing two different handles for catching the two different types of errors, you can use one to handle all of the errors that may occur in the chain.

> Always have a rejection handler at the end of a promise chain to ensure that you can properly handle any errors that may occur.

Using finally() in Promise Chains

The `finally()` method behaves differently than either `then()` or `catch()` in that it copies the state and value of the previous promise into its returned promise. That means if the original promise is fulfilled with a value, then `finally()` returns a promise that is fulfilled with the same value. For example:

```
const promise = Promise.resolve(42);

promise.finally(() => {
    console.log("Finally called.");
}).then(value => {
    console.log(value);            // 42
});
```

Here, the settlement handler can't receive the fulfilled value from `promise`, so that value is copied to a new promise that is returned from the method call. The new promise is fulfilled with the value 42 (copied from `promise`) so the fulfillment handler receives 42 as an argument. Keep in mind that even though the returned promise and `promise` have the same value, they are not the same object, as you can see in this example:

```
const promise1 = Promise.resolve(42);

const promise2 = promise1.finally(() => {
    console.log("Finally called.");
});

promise2.then(value => {
    console.log(value);         // 42
});

console.log(promise1 === promise2); // false
```

In this code, the returned value from `promise1.finally()` is stored in `promise2`, at which point you can determine that it is not the same object as `promise1`. The call to `finally()` always copies the state and value from the original promise. That also means that when `finally()` is called on a rejected promise, it in turn returns a rejected promise, as in this example:

```
const promise = Promise.reject(43);

promise.finally(() => {
    console.log("Finally called.");
}).catch(reason => {
    console.error(reason);      // 43
});
```

The promise `promise` in this example is rejected with a reason of 43. Once again, the settlement handler cannot access this information as it is not passed in as an argument, so instead it returns a new promise that is rejected for the same reason. You can then use `catch()` to retrieve the reason.

The one exception to how `finally()` works is when an error is thrown inside of the settlement handler or a rejected promise is returned. In this one case, the returned promise from `finally()` does not maintain the state and value from the original promise, and instead is rejected with the thrown error as the reason. Here's an example:

```
const promise1 = Promise.reject(43);

promise1.finally(() => {
    throw 44;
}).catch(reason => {
    console.error(reason);       // 44
});

const promise2 = Promise.reject(43);

promise2.finally(() => {
    return Promise.reject(44);
}).catch(reason => {
    console.error(reason);       // 44
});
```

Because the settlement handlers throw 44 or return `Promise.reject(44)` in this example, the returned promise is rejected with the value of 44 and that is output to the console instead of 43. The state and value of the original promise are lost as a consequence of the error being thrown in the settlement handler.

In Chapter 1, you saw how a settlement handler can be used to toggle the loading state of an application based on a call to `fetch()`. Rewriting that example using promise chains, and mixing in some error handling from earlier in this chapter, here's a complete example:

```
const appElement = document.getElementById("app");
const promise = fetch("books.json");

appElement.classList.add("loading");

promise.then(response => {
    if (response.ok) {
        console.log(response.status);
    } else {
        throw new Error(`Unexpected status code: ${
            response.status
        } ${response.statusText}`);
    }
```

```
}).finally(() => {
    appElement.classList.remove("loading");
}).catch(reason => {
    console.error(reason.message);
});
```

Unlike a try-catch statement, you don't want finally() to be the last part of the chain just in case it throws an error. So then() is called first, to handle the response from fetch(), then finally() is added to the chain to trigger the UI change, and last catch() adds the error handler for the entire chain. This is where settlement handlers passing along the state of the previous promise is helpful: if the fulfillment handler ends up throwing an error, the settlement handler will pass that rejection state along so the rejection handler can access it.

Returning Values in Promise Chains

Another important aspect of promise chains is the ability to pass data from one promise to the next. You've already seen that a value passed to the resolve() handler inside an executor is passed to the fulfillment handler for that promise. You can continue passing data along a chain by specifying a return value from the fulfillment handler. For example:

```
const promise = Promise.resolve(42);

promise.then(value => {
    console.log(value);        // 42
    return value + 1;
}).then(value => {
    console.log(value);        // 43
});
```

The fulfillment handler for promise returns value + 1 when executed. Since value is 42 (from the executor), the fulfillment handler returns 43. That value is then passed to the fulfillment handler of the second promise, which outputs it to the console.

You could do the same thing with the rejection handler. When a rejection handler is called, it may return a value. If it does, that value is used to fulfill the next promise in the chain, like this:

```
const promise = Promise.reject(42);

promise.catch(value => {
    // rejection handler
    console.error(value);      // 42
    return value + 1;
}).then(value => {
    // fulfillment handler
    console.log(value);        // 43
});
```

Here, a rejected promise is created with a value of 42. That value is passed into the rejection handler for the promise, where `value + 1` is returned. Even though this return value is coming from a rejection handler, it is still used in the fulfillment handler of the next promise in the chain. The failure of one promise can allow recovery of the entire chain if necessary.

Using `finally()`, however, results in a different behavior. Any value returned from a settlement handler is ignored so that you can access the original promise's value. Here's an example:

```
const promise = Promise.resolve(42);

promise.finally(() => {
    // settlement handler
    return 43;                      // ignored!
}).then(value => {
    // fulfillment handler
    console.log(value);        // 42
});
```

The `value` passed to the fulfillment handler is 42 and not 43. The `return` statement in the settlement handler is ignored so that the original value can be retrieved using `then()`. This is one of the consequences of `finally()` returning a promise whose state and value are copied from the original.

Returning Promises in Promise Chains

Returning primitive values from promise handlers allows passing of data between promises, but what if you return an object? If the object is a promise, then there's an extra step that's taken to determine how to proceed. Consider the following example:

```
const promise1 = Promise.resolve(42);
const promise2 = Promise.resolve(43);

promise1.then(value => {
    console.log(value);     // 42
    return promise2;
}).then(value => {
    console.log(value);     // 43
});
```

In this code, `promise1` resolves to 42. The fulfillment handler for `promise1` returns `promise2`, a promise already in the resolved state. The second fulfillment handler is called because `promise2` has been fulfilled. If `promise2` were rejected, a rejection handler (if present) would be called instead of the second fulfillment handler.

The important thing to recognize about this pattern is that the second fulfillment handler is not added to `promise2`, but rather to a third promise, making the previous example equivalent to this:

```
const promise1 = Promise.resolve(42);
const promise2 = Promise.resolve(43);

const promise3 = promise1.then(value => {
    console.log(value);     // 42
    return promise2;
});

promise3.then(value => {
    console.log(value);     // 43
});
```

Here, it's clear that the second fulfillment handler is attached to `promise3` rather than `promise2`. This is a subtle but important distinction, as the second fulfillment handler will not be called if `promise2` is rejected. For instance:

```
const promise1 = Promise.resolve(42);
const promise2 = Promise.reject(43);

promise1.then(value => {
    console.log(value);     // 42
    return promise2;
}).then(value => {
    console.log(value);     // never called
});
```

In this example, the second fulfillment handler is never called because `promise2` is rejected. You could, however, attach a rejection handler instead:

```
const promise1 = Promise.resolve(42);
const promise2 = Promise.reject(43);

promise1.then(value => {
    console.log(value);     // 42
    return promise2;
}).catch(value => {
    console.error(value);   // 43
});
```

Here, the rejection handler is called as a result of `promise2` being rejected. The rejected value 43 from `promise2` is passed into that rejection handler.

Returning a promise from a fulfillment handler is helpful when an operation requires more than one promise to execute to completion. For example, `fetch()` requires a second promise to read the body of a response. To read a JSON body, you'll need to use `response.json()`, which returns another promise. Here's how it looks without using promise chaining:

```
const promise1 = fetch("books.json");

promise1.then(response => {

    promise2 = response.json();
    promise2.then(payload => {
        console.log(payload);
    }).catch(reason => {
        console.error(reason.message);
    });

}).catch(reason => {
    console.error(reason.message);
});
```

This code requires two different rejection handlers to catch the potential errors at two different steps of the process. Returning the second promise from the first fulfillment handler simplifies the code:

```
const promise = fetch("books.json");

promise.then(response => {
    return response.json();
}).then(payload => {
    console.log(payload);
}).catch(reason => {
    console.error(reason.message);
});
```

Here, the first fulfillment handler is called when a response is received and then returns a promise to read the response body as JSON. The second fulfillment handler is called when the body has been read and the payload is ready to be used. You need only one rejection handler at the end of the promise chain to catch errors that occur along the way.

Returning a promise from a settlement handler using `finally()` also exhibits some different behavior than using `then()` or `catch()`. First, if you return a fulfilled promise from a settlement handler, then that promise is ignored in favor of the value from the original promise, as in this example:

```
const promise = Promise.resolve(42);

promise.finally(() => {
    return Promise.resolve(44);
}).then(value => {
    console.log(value);     // 42
});
```

In this example, the settlement handler returns a promise that is fulfilled with 44, but the returned promise is fulfilled with the original promise's value, which is 42.

However, if you return a rejected promise from a settlement handler, then the returned promise adopts that reason and the returned promise is rejected, like this:

```
const promise = Promise.resolve(42);

promise.finally(() => {
    return Promise.reject(43);
}).catch(reason => {
    console.error(reason);   // 43
});
```

This holds true even if the original promise is rejected, as in this example:

```
const promise = Promise.reject(43);

promise.finally(() => {
    return Promise.reject(45);
}).catch(reason => {
    console.log(reason);    // 45
});
```

Returning a rejected promise from a settlement handler is functionally equivalent to throwing an error: the returned promise is rejected with the specified reason.

Returning promises from fulfillment or rejection handlers doesn't change when the promise executors are executed. The first defined promise will run its executor first; then the second promise executor will run, and so on. Returning promises simply allows you to define additional responses to the promise results. You defer the execution of fulfillment handlers by creating a new promise within a fulfillment handler. For example:

```
const p1 = Promise.resolve(42);

p1.then(value => {
    console.log(value);     // 42

    // create a new promise
    const p2 = new Promise((resolve, reject) => {
        setTimeout(() => {
            resolve(43);
        }, 500);
    });

    return p2;
}).then(value => {
    console.log(value);     // 43
});
```

In this example, a new promise is created within the fulfillment handler for p1. That means the second fulfillment handler won't execute until after p2 is fulfilled. The executor for p2 resolves the promise after 500 milliseconds using setTimeout(), but more realistically you might make a network or file system request. This pattern is useful when you want to wait until a previous promise has been settled before starting a new asynchronous operation.

Summary

Multiple promises can be chained together in a variety of ways to pass information between them. Each call to `then()`, `catch()`, and `finally()` creates and returns a new promise that is resolved when the preceding promise is settled. If the promise handler returns a value, then that value becomes the value of the newly created promise from `then()` and `catch()` (`finally()` ignores this value); if the promise handler throws an error, then the error is caught and the returned newly created promise is rejected using that error as the reason.

When one promise is rejected in a chain, the promises created from other chained handlers are also rejected until the end of the chain is reached. Knowing this, it's recommended to attach a rejection handler at the end of each promise chain to ensure that errors are handled correctly. Failing to catch a promise rejection will result in a message being output to the console, an error being thrown, or both (depending on the runtime environment).

You can return promises from handlers, and in that case, the promise returned from the call to `then()` and `catch()` will settle to match the settlement state and value of the promise returned from the handler (fulfilled promises returned from `finally()` are ignored while rejected promises are honored). You can use this to your advantage by delaying some operations until a promise is fulfilled, then initiating and returning a second promise to continue using the same promise chain.

This chapter explored how to chain multiple promises together so they act more like one promise. In this next chapter, you'll learn how to work with multiple promises acting in parallel.

3. Working with Multiple Promises

Up to this point, each example in this book has dealt with responding to one promise at a time. Sometimes, however, you'll want to monitor the progress of multiple promises in order to determine the next action. JavaScript provides several methods that monitor multiple promises and respond to them in slightly different ways. All of the methods discussed in this chapter allow multiple promises to be executed in parallel and then responded to as a group rather than individually.

The Promise.all() Method

The `Promise.all()` method accepts a single argument, which is an iterable (such as an array) of promises to monitor, and returns a promise that is resolved only when every promise in the iterable is resolved. The returned promise is fulfilled when every promise in the iterable is fulfilled, as in this example:

```
let promise1 = Promise.resolve(42);

let promise2 = new Promise((resolve, reject) => {
    resolve(43);
});

let promise3 = new Promise((resolve, reject) => {
    setTimeout(() => {
        resolve(44);
    }, 100);
});
```

```
let promise4 = Promise.all([promise1, promise2, promise3]);

promise4.then(value => {
    console.log(Array.isArray(value));    // true
    console.log(value[0]);                // 42
    console.log(value[1]);                // 43
    console.log(value[2]);                // 44
});
```

Each promise here resolves with a number. The call to `Promise.all()` creates promise `promise4`, which is ultimately fulfilled when promises `promise1`, `promise2`, and `promise3` are fulfilled. The result passed to the fulfillment handler for `promise4` is an array containing each resolved value: 42, 43, and 44. The values are stored in the order the promises were passed to `Promise.all()`, so you can match promise results to the promises that resolved to them.

If any promise passed to `Promise.all()` is rejected, the returned promise is immediately rejected without waiting for the other promises to complete:

```
let promise1 = Promise.resolve(42);

let promise2 = Promise.reject(43);

let promise3 = new Promise((resolve, reject) => {
    setTimeout(() => {
        resolve(44);
    }, 100);
});

let promise4 = Promise.all([promise1, promise2, promise3]);

promise4.catch(reason => {
    console.log(Array.isArray(reason));   // false
    console.log(reason);                  // 43
});
```

In this example, the second promise (`promise2`) is rejected with a value of 43. The rejection handler for `promise4` is called immediately without waiting for the first promise (promise1) or third promise (promise3) to finish executing. (They do still finish executing; promise4 just doesn't wait.)

The rejection handler always receives a single value rather than an array, and the value is the rejection value from the promise that was rejected. In this case, the rejection handler is passed 43 to reflect the rejection from promise2.

> Any non-promise value in the iterable argument is passed to Promise.resolve() to convert it into a promise.

When to Use Promise.all()

You'll want to use Promise.all() in any situation where you are waiting for multiple promises to fulfill, and any one failure should cause the entire operation to fail. Here are some common use cases for Promise.all().

Processing Multiple Files Together

When using a server-side JavaScript runtime such as Node.js or Deno, you may need to read from multiple files to work with data contained inside. In this situation, it's most efficient to read files in parallel and wait until they've all been read before proceeding to process the data you've retrieved. Here's an example that works in Node.js:

```
import { readFile } from "node:fs/promises";

function readFiles(filenames) {
    return Promise.all(
        filenames.map(filename => readFile(filename, "utf8"))
    );
}

readFiles([
    "file1.json",
    "file2.json"
]).then(fileContents => {
```

```
    // parse JSON data
    const data = fileContents.map(
        fileContent => JSON.parse(fileContent)
    );

    // process as necessary
    console.log(data);

}).catch(reason => {
    console.error(reason.message);
});
```

This example uses the Node.js promises-based filesystem API to read multiple files in parallel. The `readFiles()` function accepts an array of filenames to read and then maps each filename to a promise created by the imported `readFile()` function. The file is read as text (as indicated by the `"utf8"` encoding passed as the second argument), and the results are available in the fulfillment handler as the `fileContents` array, which contains the text of each filename. From that point, the file contents are parsed as JSON into the `data` array and then passed to the `processData()` function. This is a common way to process data across multiple files because if any one file cannot be read or parsed, then the operation cannot be completed correctly and should be stopped.

Calling Multiple Dependent Web Service APIs

Another common use case for `Promise.all()` is when calling multiple web service APIs. This is especially common with REST APIs where each type of data associated with an entity may have its own endpoints. For example, consider an application where each user has both blog posts and albums, and you may need to gather all of that information on the user's profile. The code might look like this:

```
const API_BASE = "https://jsonplaceholder.typicode.com";

function createError(response) {
    return new Error(`Unexpected status code: ${
        response.status
    } ${response.statusText} for ${response.url}`);
}
```

```javascript
function fetchUserData(userId) {

    const urls = [
        `${API_BASE}/users/${userId}/posts`,
        `${API_BASE}/users/${userId}/albums`
    ];

    return Promise.all(urls.map(url => fetch(url)));
}

fetchUserData(1).then(responses => {
    return Promise.all(
        responses.map(
            response => {
                if (response.ok) {
                    return response.json();
                } else {
                    return Promise.reject(
                        createError(response)
                    );
                }
            }
        )
    );
}).then(([posts, albums]) => {

    // process your data as necessary
    console.log(posts);
    console.log(albums);

}).catch(reason => console.error(reason.message));
```

This example uses the JSONPlaceholder[1] service, which is a free fake API for testing and prototyping. Given a particular user ID, JSONPlaceholder will generate fake data. In this case, the code is using the `/posts` and `/albums` endpoints for each user. The `fetchUserData()` function accepts a user ID and generates the URLs to call. Then the URLs are mapped to the promise returned by each `fetch()` call. When the responses are retrieved, another `Promise.all()` call is used to map each response to another promise, either the JSON body if the response was in the 200-

299 range or a rejected promise otherwise (which will short-circuit the entire operation and call the rejection handler). In the last fulfillment handler, the posts and albums data is available to be processed.

Creating Artificial Delays

A less common scenario for Promise.all() is when you want to delay something from happening too quickly. This is more likely to happen in a browser rather than on the server-side, where you sometimes need a slight delay between a user action and the response. For example, you may want to display a loading indicator when fetching data from the server, but if the response is too fast, the user may not see the loading spinner and therefore not know that the data on the screen is the most recent. In such a situation, you can introduce an artificial delay, like this:

```
const API_BASE = "https://jsonplaceholder.typicode.com";
const appElement = document.getElementById("app");

function createError(response) {
    return new Error(`Unexpected status code: ${
        response.status
    } ${response.statusText} for ${response.url}`);
}

function delay(milliseconds) {
    return new Promise(resolve => {
        setTimeout(() => {
            resolve();
        }, milliseconds);
    });
}

function fetchUserData(userId) {

    appElement.classList.add("loading");

    const urls = [
        `${API_BASE}/users/${userId}/posts`,
        `${API_BASE}/users/${userId}/albums`
    ];
```

```
    return Promise.all([
        ...urls.map(url => fetch(url)),
        delay(1500)
    ]).then(results => {
        // strip off the undefined result from delay()
        return results.slice(0, results.length - 1);
    });
}

fetchUserData(1).then(responses => {
    return Promise.all(
        responses.map(
            response => {
                if (response.ok) {
                    return response.json();
                } else {
                    return Promise.reject(
                        createError(response)
                    );
                }
            }
        )
    );
}).then(([posts, albums]) => {

    // process your data as necessary
    console.log(posts);
    console.log(albums);

}).finally(() => {
    appElement.classList.remove("loading");
}).catch(reason => console.error(reason.message));
```

This code builds on the preceding example by introducing a delay into each `fetch()` call. The `delay()` function returns a promise that resolves after a specified number of milliseconds have passed. It does so by using the native `setTimeout()` function and passing a callback function that calls `resolve()`. Note that there is no need to pass any value to `resolve()` in this situation because there is no relevant data.

> You could also pass `resolve` directly as the first argument to `setTimeout()`; however, some JavaScript runtimes pass an argument to the timeout callback. For best compatibility across runtimes, it's best to call `resolve()` from inside of another function.

The `fetchUserData()` function initiates the web service requests for the specified user ID. As in the example from the previous section, `Promise.all()` is used to monitor multiple `fetch()` requests, but in this example, there is also a call to `delay()` included in the array passed to `Promise.all()`. When the returned promise is fulfilled, the fulfillment handler receives an array of all results, including `undefined` as the last array element. Before returning from `fetchUserData()`, that last element is removed so that the code calling `fetchUserData()` doesn't need to be aware of the `delay()` call at all. The CSS class `loading` is added to the application element in the DOM to indicate that data is being retrieved and is later removed by a settlement handler when a response is received.

You've just learned use cases where using `Promise.all()` is the best solution. But what if you want your operation to continue even if one promise is rejected? That's where `Promise.allSettled()` is the better choice.

The Promise.allSettled() Method

The `Promise.allSettled()` method is a slight variation of `Promise.all()` where the method waits until all promises in the specified iterable are settled, regardless of whether they are fulfilled or rejected. The return value of `Promise.allSettled()` is always a promise that is fulfilled with an array of result objects.

The result object for a fulfilled promise has two properties:

- `status` - always set to the string `fulfilled`
- `value` - the fulfillment value of the promise

For a rejected promise, there are also two properties on the result object:

- `status` - always set to the string `rejected`
- `reason` - the rejection value of the promise

You can use the returned array of result objects to determine the result of each individual promise.

```
let promise1 = Promise.resolve(42);

let promise2 = Promise.reject(43);

let promise3 = new Promise((resolve, reject) => {
    setTimeout(() => {
        resolve(44);
    }, 100);
});

let promise4 = Promise.allSettled([promise1, promise2, promise3]);

promise4.then(results => {
    console.log(Array.isArray(results));     // true

    console.log(results[0].status);          // "fulfilled"
    console.log(results[0].value);           // 42

    console.log(results[1].status);          // "rejected"
    console.log(results[1].reason);          // 43

    console.log(results[2].status);          // "fulfilled"
    console.log(results[2].value);           // 44
});
```

Even though the second promise (`promise2`) is a rejected promise, the call to `Promise.allSettled()` returns a fulfilled promise with an array of result objects. You can then look through the result objects to determine the outcome of each promise.

When to Use Promise.allSettled()

The `Promise.allSettled()` method can be used in a lot of the same situations as `Promise.all()`; however, it is best suited for when you want to ignore rejections, handle rejections differently, or allow partial success. Here are some common use cases for `Promise.allSettled()`.

Processing Multiple Files Separately

When discussing `Promise.all()`, you saw an example of working on multiple files that were dependent on one another to succeed. There are also some cases where working on multiple files separately means you don't need to stop the entire operation if one fails; you go ahead and complete the successful operations and then log the failed ones to retry later. Here's an example in Node.js:

```
import { readFile, writeFile } from "node:fs/promises";

// or any operation on the files
function transformText(text) {
    return text.split("").reverse().join("");
}

function transformFiles(filenames) {
    return Promise.allSettled(
        filenames.map(filename =>
            readFile(filename, "utf8")
                .then(text => transformText(text))
                .then(newText => writeFile(filename, newText))
                .catch(reason => {
                    reason.filename = filename;
                    return Promise.reject(reason);
                })
        )
    );
}

transformFiles([
    "file1.txt",
    "file2.txt"
]).then(results => {

    // get failed results
    const failedResults = results.filter(
        result => result.status === "rejected"
    );
```

```
        if (failedResults.length) {
            console.error("Files not transformed:");
            console.error("");

            failedResults.forEach(failedResult => {
                console.error(failedResult.reason.filename);
                console.error(failedResult.reason.message);
                console.error("");
            });
        } else {
            console.log("All files transformed.");
        }

});
```

This example reads in a series of files, reverses the order of the text in the files, and then writes that text back to the original files (you can, of course, replace transformText() with whatever operation you would prefer). The transformFiles() function accepts an array of filenames and reads the contents of the file, transforms the text, and writes the transformed text back to the file. The promise chain represents each step in the process, and the rejection handler adds a filename property to any rejection reason to make it easier to interpret the results after the fact.

When the operation on all of the files is completed, the results are filtered to find any files where the transform did not complete successfully and then outputs those results to the console. In a production system you would likely feed the failed results into a monitoring system or a queue to try the transformation again.

Calling Multiple Independent Web Service APIs

Another example from the Promise.all() section was calling multiple web service APIs where you wanted all of the requests to succeed. If you don't need all of the requests to succeed, then you can use Promise.allSettled() instead. Going back to that previous example, if it's possible to display the user profile page, even if some of the data is missing, then use Promise.allSettled() instead of Promise.all() to avoid showing an error to the user. For example:

```
const API_BASE = "https://jsonplaceholder.typicode.com";

function fetchUserData(userId) {

    const urls = [
        `${API_BASE}/users/${userId}/posts`,
        `${API_BASE}/users/${userId}/albums`,
        `${API_BASE}/users/${userId}/extras`
    ];

    return Promise.allSettled(urls.map(url => fetch(url)))
        .then(results => results.map(result => result.value));
}

fetchUserData(1).then(responses => {
    return Promise.all(
        responses.map(
            response => {
                if (response?.ok) {
                    return response.json();
                }
            }
        )
    );
}).then(([posts, albums, extras]) => {

    // process your data as necessary
    if (posts) {
        console.log("Posts");
        console.log(posts);
    }

    if (albums) {
        console.log("Albums");
        console.log(albums);
    }
```

```
    if (extras) {
        console.log("Extras");
        console.log(extras);
    }

}).catch(reason => console.error(reason.message));
```

In this version of the example, the `fetchUserData()` function uses `Promise.allSettled()` instead of `Promise.all()` to ensure that rejections can be ignored. This example also calls a third endpoint, `/users/{userId}/extras`, which doesn't exist and will return a 404 (for demonstration purposes). Once all requests have completed, a fulfillment handler maps each result to its `value` property, which ensures that any rejected promises are mapped to `undefined` and fulfilled promises are mapped to the response object returned from `fetch()`.

Because `response` may be `undefined`, you need to check that `response` is a truthy before checking the `ok` property. The JSON body of each valid response is then read, and the last fulfillment handler reads that data. There is no guarantee that each of the requested data will be there (`extras` will be `undefined` in this example) so you need to check that each value is present before processing it.

Waiting for Animations to Finish

In a web page, elements can be animated in a number of different ways simultaneously. You could, for instance, animate the location of an element up from the bottom of the page while also animating the width and height to grow the element into view. It's helpful in these situations to wait for all animations to complete before making the next modification to the element or page. In his article, *Building a toast component*[2], Adam Argyle explained a basic way to track when the animations of a DOM element are complete. I've rewritten the code for clarity here:

```
function waitForAnimations(element) {
    return Promise.allSettled(
        element.getAnimations().map(animation => animation.finished)
    );
}

const toasterElement = document.getElementById("toaster");
```

```
waitForAnimations(toasterElement)
    .then(() => console.log("Toaster is done."));
```

In this case, you don't really care if any of the animations fail along the way, nor do you care about receiving any fulfilled values from the animations, so `Promise.allSettled()` is a more appropriate option than `Promise.all()`. The `getAnimations()` method returns an array of animation objects, each of which has a `finished` property containing a promise that is resolved when the animation is complete. By passing each of these promises into `Promise.allSettled()`, you will be notified when all animations are complete. Because `Promise.allSettled()` never returns a rejected promise, you can just attach a fulfillment handler and not be worried about any uncaught rejection errors.

The Promise.any() Method

The `Promise.any()` method also accepts an iterable of promises and returns a fulfilled promise when any of the passed-in promises are fulfilled. The operation short-circuits as soon as one of the promises is fulfilled. (This is the opposite of `Promise.all()`, where the operation short-circuits as soon as one promise is rejected.) Here's an example:

```
let promise1 = Promise.reject(43);

let promise2 = Promise.resolve(42);

let promise3 = new Promise((resolve, reject) => {
    setTimeout(() => {
        resolve(44);
    }, 100);
});

let promise4 = Promise.any([promise1, promise2, promise3]);

promise4.then(value => console.log(value));                      // 42
```

Even though the first promise (`promise1`) in this example is rejected, the call to `Promise.any()` succeeds because the second promise (`promise2`) is fulfilled. The result of the third promise (`promise3`) is discarded.

If all of the promises passed to `Promise.any()` are rejected, then the returned promise is rejected with an `AggregateError`. An `AggregateError` is an error that represents multiple errors stored in an `errors` property. For example:

```
let promise1 = Promise.reject(43);

let promise2 = new Promise((resolve, reject) => {
    reject(44);
});

let promise3 = new Promise((resolve, reject) => {
    setTimeout(() => {
        reject(45);
    }, 100);
});

let promise4 = Promise.any([promise1, promise2, promise3]);

promise4.catch(reason => {
    // Runtime dependent error message
    console.log(reason.message);

    // output rejection values
    console.log(reason.errors[0]);   // 43
    console.log(reason.errors[1]);   // 44
    console.log(reason.errors[2]);   // 45
});
```

Here, `Promise.any()` receives promises that are not fulfilled, and so the returned promise is rejected with an `AggregateError`. You can inspect the `errors` property, which is an array, to retrieve the rejection values from each promise.

When to Use Promise.any()

The `Promise.any()` method is best used in situations where you want any one of the promises to fulfill and you don't care how many others reject unless they all reject. Here are some situations where you might want to use `Promise.any()`.

Executing Hedged Requests

As defined in *The Tail at Scale*[3], a *hedged request* is one where the client makes requests to multiple servers and accepts the response from the first that replies. This is helpful in situations where the client needs the lowest latency possible, and there are server resources devoted to managing the extra load and deduplicating responses. Here's an example:

```
const HOSTS = [
    "api1.example.com",
    "api2.example.com"
];

function hedgedFetch(endpoint) {
    return Promise.any(
        HOSTS.map(hostname => fetch(`https://${hostname}${endpoint}`))
    );
}

hedgedFetch("/transactions")
    .then(transactions => console.log(transations))
    .catch(reason => console.error(reason.message));
```

This example keeps an array of hosts that should be called for each hedged request. The `hedgedFetch()` function creates an array of `fetch()` requests based on those hostnames and passes that array to `Promise.any()`. To the consumer of `hedgedFetch()`, it looks as if just one request is made even though multiple are happening behind the scenes. This allows the consumer to use just one fulfillment handler and one rejection handler to handle the result. If any one of the requests fails, the consumer is never aware; the rejection handler is only called if all requests fail.

Using the Fastest Response in a Service Worker

Web pages that use service workers often have their choice of where to load data from: the network or from the cache. In some cases, a network request might actually be faster than loading from cache, and so you may want to use `Promise.any()` to choose the faster of the responses. Here's some code that illustrates this pattern inside of a service worker:

```
self.addEventListener("fetch", event => {

    // get cached response
    const cachedResponse = caches.match(event.request);

    // fetch new response
    const fetchedResponse = fetch(event.request.url);

    // respond with the best option
    event.respondWith(
        Promise.any([
            fetchedResponse.catch(() => cachedResponse),
            cachedResponse,
        ])
            .then(response => response ?? fetchedResponse)
            .catch(() => {})
    );

});
```

The fetch event listener allows you to listen for network requests and intercept the responses. This service worker example uses a fetch event listener to read both from the cache (using caches.match()) and from the network (using fetch()). The call to caches.match() returns a promise that is always fulfilled, either with the matching response object or with undefined if the request isn't in the cache. The event.respondWith() method expects a promise to be passed, so this event handler passes the result of Promise.any().

Two promises are passed to Promise.any(): the fetched response with a rejection handler that defaults back to the cached response and the cached response itself. In this way, the cached response is returned both if there is a cache hit that fulfills first and if the fetched response is rejected. The fulfillment handler then makes sure there is a valid response (remember, response might be undefined if the cache responds first with a miss). The rejection handler doesn't do anything because there is no fallback in this situation. Both the fetched response and the cached response were rejected, so the error is silently ignored to allow the browser to use its default behavior.

While Promise.any() short-circuits after the first fulfilled promise, you may also want to short-circuit the operation based on the first settled promise regardless of the outcome. For that case, you can use `Promise.race()` (discussed later in this chapter).

The Promise.race() Method

The `Promise.race()` method provides a slightly different take on monitoring multiple promises. This method also accepts an iterable of promises to monitor and returns a promise, but the returned promise is settled as soon as the first promise is settled. Instead of waiting for all promises to be resolved like the `Promise.all()` method or short-circuiting only for the first resolved promise like `Promise.any()`, the `Promise.race()` method returns an appropriate promise as soon as any promise in the array is settled. For example:

```
let promise1 = Promise.resolve(42);

let promise2 = new Promise((resolve, reject) => {
    resolve(43);
});

let promise3 = new Promise((resolve, reject) => {
    setTimeout(() => {
        resolve(44);
    }, 100);
});

let promise4 = Promise.race([promise1, promise2, promise3]);

promise4.then(value => console.log(value));     // 42
```

In this code, the first promise (`promise1`) is created as a fulfilled promise while the others schedule jobs. The fulfillment handler for `promise4` is then called with the value of 42 and ignores the other promises. The promises passed to `Promise.race()` are truly in a race to see which is settled first. If the first promise to settle is fulfilled, then the returned promise is fulfilled; if the first promise to settle is rejected, then the returned promise is rejected. Here's an example with a rejection:

```
let promise1 = new Promise((resolve, reject) => {
    setTimeout(() => {
        resolve(42);
    }, 100);
});

let promise2 = new Promise((resolve, reject) => {
    reject(43);
});

let promise3 = new Promise((resolve, reject) => {
    setTimeout(() => {
        resolve(44);
    }, 50);
});

let promise4 = Promise.race([promise1, promise2, promise3]);

promise4.catch(reason => console.log(reason));        // 43
```

Here, both `promise1` and `promise3` use `setTimeout()` to delay promise fulfillment. The result is that `promise4` is rejected because `promise2` is rejected before either `promise1` or `promise3` is resolved. Even though `promise1` and `promise3` are eventually fulfilled, those results are ignored because they occur after `promise2` is rejected.

When to Use Promise.race()

The `Promise.race()` method is best used in situations where you want to be able to short-circuit the completion of a number of different promises. Unlike `Promise.any()`, where you specifically want one of the promises to succeed and only care if all promises fail, with `Promise.race()` you want to know even if one promise fails as long as it fails before any other promise fulfills. Here are some situations where you may want to use `Promise.race()`.

Establishing a Timeout for an Operation

While the `fetch()` function has a lot of helpful functionality, one thing it doesn't do is manage a timeout for a given request; a request will happily hang until the request completes one way or another. You can easily create a wrapper method to add a timeout to any request by using `Promise.race()`:

```
function timeout(milliseconds) {
    return new Promise((resolve, reject) => {
        setTimeout(() => {
            reject(new Error("Request timed out."));
        }, milliseconds);
    });
}

function fetchWithTimeout(...args) {
    return Promise.race([
        fetch(...args),
        timeout(5000)
    ]);
}

const API_URL = "https://jsonplaceholder.typicode.com/users";

fetchWithTimeout(API_URL)
    .then(response => response.json())
    .then(users => console.log(users))
    .catch(reason => console.error(reason.message));
```

The `timeout()` function is similar to the `delay()` function created earlier in this chapter except that it calls `reject()` after a delay rather than `resolve()`. In this case, the delay represents an error condition as you want to be informed when a request has taken longer than expected (5000 milliseconds in this example). The `fetchWithTimeout()` function then calls `fetch()` along with `timeout()` in an array that is passed to `Promise.race()`. If the call to `fetch()` takes longer than the timeout, the returned promise is rejected so you can handle the failure appropriately.

> Keep in mind that even though `fetchWithTimeout()` will reject if a request takes longer than the specified timeout, the request will not be cancelled. It will continue waiting for a response behind-the-scenes even though the response will be ignored.

Summary

For times when you want to monitor and respond to multiple promises at the same time, JavaScript provides several methods. Each method behaves slightly differently, but all allow you to run promises in parallel and respond to them as a group:

- `Promise.all()` - the returned promise is fulfilled when all of the promises are fulfilled, and the returned promise is rejected when any promise is rejected.
- `Promise.allSettled()` - the returned promise is always fulfilled with an array of results from the promise, and the returned promise is never rejected.
- `Promise.any()` - the returned promise is fulfilled when the first promise is fulfilled, and the returned promise is rejected when all of the promises are rejected.
- `Promise.race()` - the returned promise is fulfilled when the first promise to settle is fulfilled, and the returned promise is rejected when the first promise to settle is rejected.

Each of these methods is appropriate for different use cases, and it's up to you to decide which is appropriate in any situation.

---

1. https://jsonplaceholder.typicode.com/
2. https://web.dev/building-a-toast-component/
3. https://www.barroso.org/publications/TheTailAtScale.pdf

4. Async Functions and Await Expressions

JavaScript promises were designed to be a low-level utility that could be used behind-the-scenes by higher-level language features. Async functions are just such a higher-level language feature that makes programming with promises more similar to programming without promises. Instead of worry about tracking promises and their various handlers, async functions abstract away the promises. The end result is code that follows a familiar top-down sequence.

Before getting into the details of how async functions work, it helps to understand how they are defined.

> I use the term "async functions" to describe functions as well as methods that appear on objects or classes. Whenever the term is used, you can assume what I'm saying also applies to asynchronous methods unless otherwise indicated.

Defining Async Functions

Async functions can be used anywhere synchronous functions can be used. In most cases, all you need to do is add the `async` keyword before any function or method definition to make it asynchronous. Here are some examples:

```js
// async function declaration
async function doSomething() {
    // body
}

// async arrow function
const doSomethingToo = async () => {
    // body
};

// async arrow function
const doSomethingElse = async a => {
    // body
};

// async object method
const object = {
    async doSomething() {
        // body
    }
};

// async class method
class MyClass {
    async doSomething() {
        // body
    }
}
```

The async keyword indicates that the following function or method should be made asynchronous. It's important for the JavaScript engine to know ahead of time if a function is asynchronous because it behaves differently than a synchronous function.

What Makes Async Functions Different

Async functions are different from synchronous functions in four ways:

1. The return value is always a promise
2. Thrown errors are promise rejections
3. The `await` expression can be used
4. The `for-await-of` loop can be used

These four aspects of async functions make them quite different from synchronous functions, so it's worth going through each point in more detail.

The Return Value Is Always a Promise

You can use the `return` operator in async functions the same as synchronous functions. The difference is that async functions always return a promise regardless of the type of value you specify with `return`. If you return a number, for example, that number is wrapped in a promise:

```
async function getMeaningOfLife() {
    return 42;
}

const result = getMeaningOfLife();
console.log(result instanceof Promise);     // true
console.log(typeof result === "number");    // false

result.then(value => {
    console.log(value);                     // 42
});
```

In this code, the `getMeaningOfLife()` async function returns the number 42, but the return value is actually a fulfilled promise. You can then attach a fulfillment handler to retrieve the value. Effectively, async functions call `Promise.resolve()` behind-the-scenes to ensure a promise is always returned.

If you pass a promise to `return` inside of an async function, then that promise is not passed through directly. Instead, the promise state and value are copied to a new promise and returned. Here's an example:

```
const promise = Promise.resolve(42);

async function getMeaningOfLife() {
    return promise;
}

const result = getMeaningOfLife();
console.log(result === promise);    // false
result.then(value => {
    console.log(value);             // 42
});
```

Here, `result` is not the same promise object as `promise`, but it does have all of the same internal state and so still resolves to 42.

If you don't specify a return value for an async function, then the return value is a promise that resolves to `undefined`. For example:

```
async function doSomething() {
    // no return value
}

const result = doSomething();
console.log(result instanceof Promise); // true
result.then(value => {
    console.log(value);                 // undefined
});
```

The bottom line is no matter what you do inside an async function, it will always return a promise. That is also the case when an error is thrown.

Thrown Errors Are Promise Rejections

When an error is thrown in an async function, a rejected promise is returned instead of throwing the error outside the function. That means you cannot catch errors from async functions using `try-catch`. For example, the following will not trap the error:

```
async function throwError() {
    throw new Error("Oh no!");
}

try {
    throwError();
    console.log("Didn't catch error");
} catch (ex) {
    // never called
    console.log("Caught error");
}
```

In this example, the `try-catch` statement doesn't catch the error thrown by `throwError()` because a rejected promise is returned. To catch the error, you need to provide a rejection handler, like this:

```
async function throwError() {
    throw new Error("Oh no!");
}

throwError().catch(reason => {
    console.log("Caught error:", reason.message);
});
```

Here, the rejection handler is assigned using `catch()`, and the error results in a message being output to the console.

The JavaScript engine goes through a lot of trouble to ensure that async functions always return promises so you have a consistent way to work with the return value. That brings us to the third way that async functions are different from synchronous functions: the `await` expression.

Using Await Expressions

The `await` expression is designed to make working with promises simple. Instead of manually assigning fulfillment and rejection handlers, any promise used in an `await` expression behaves more like code in a synchronous function: the expression returns the fulfilled value of a promise when it succeeds and throws the rejection value when the promise fails. That allows you to easily assign the result of an `await` expression to a variable and catch any rejections using a try-catch statement. Here's an example using the fetch() API (available in web browsers and Deno) without await:

```
function retrieveJsonData(url) {
    return fetch(url)
        .then(response => {
            if (response.ok) {
                return response.json();
            } else {
                throw new Error(`Unexpected status code: ${
                    response.status
                } ${response.statusText}`);
            }
        })
        .catch(reason => console.error(reason.message));
}
```

The retrieveJsonData() function returns a promise that resolves to the JSON data in the response from the call to fetch(). There is also a rejection handler to print out any error messages. Here's how you can rewrite this function as an async function that uses await:

```
async function retrieveJsonData(url) {

    try {
        const response = await fetch(url);
        if (response.ok) {
            return await response.json();
        } else {
            throw new Error(`Unexpected status code: ${
                response.status
            } ${response.statusText}`);
        }
    } catch (error) {
        console.error(error.message);
    }
}
```

In this rewritten version of retrieveJsonData(), the call to await fetch(url) handles defining fulfillment and rejection handlers for the returned promise. The variable response is assigned the fulfillment value of that promise (if successful), and rejection throws an error that is caught by the try-catch statement. The function still returns a promise that resolves to the JSON data, but it does so by returning the fulfillment value of response.json() (another promise). If a rejection is triggered in response.json(), then that is also thrown as an error and caught in the try-catch statement.

You may be wondering why not return `response.json()` directly without `await` if it is a promise? For example:

```
async function retrieveJsonData(url) {

    try {
        const response = await fetch(url);
        if (response.ok) {
            return response.json();
        } else {
            throw new Error(`Unexpected status code: ${
                response.status
            } ${response.statusText}`);
        }
    } catch (error) {
        console.error(error.message);
    }
}
```

This will work the same as the preceding example when `response.json()` succeeds; when `response.json()` fails, however, that rejection will not be thrown as an error and therefore will not be caught with the `try-catch` in this function. It's the `await` expression that causes rejections to be thrown as errors, so if you omit `await`, the promise rejection will only be caught by a rejection handler. In this example, the rejection handler would have to be added by the code calling this function, like this:

```
async function retrieveJsonData(url) {

    try {
        const response = await fetch(url);
        if (response.ok) {
            return response.json();
        } else {
            throw new Error(`Unexpected status code: ${
                response.status
            } ${response.statusText}`);
        }
```

```
        } catch (error) {
            console.error(error.message);
        }
    }

    retrieveJsonData("https://api.example.com/users")
        .then(data => doSomething(data))
        .catch(reason => console.error(reason.message));
```

There are valid use cases for both scenarios, some where you want to catch the error inside of the async function and some where you want the error to flow outside the function.

Using Await Expressions with Non-Promises

You can also use `await` with non-promise values because the value is always passed through `Promise.resolve()`. That means promises are passed through directly, non-promise thenables are resolved to promises, and other values are wrapped in promises. For example:

```
async function getMeaningOfLife() {
    return await 42;
};

getMeaningOfLife().then(value => console.log(value));
```

The `getMeaningOfLife()` function in this code returns a promise that is fulfilled with the value 42. You can achieve the same functionality without an async function by rewriting the previous example as follows:

```
function getMeaningOfLife() {
    return Promise.resolve(42);
};

getMeaningOfLife().then(value => console.log(value));
```

The ability of `await` to handle non-promise values means that you aren't penalized if you guess incorrectly about the value being used.

Using Await Expressions with Multiple Promises

Even though `await` expressions operate on a single promise, you can take advantage of the built-in promise methods to effectively operate on multiple promises. For example, if you'd like to wait for every promise in an array to be fulfilled, you can use the `Promise.all()` method with an `await`:

```
async function doSomething() {

    try {
        return await Promise.all([
            promise1,
            promise2,
            promise3
        ]);
    } catch (error) {
        console.error(error.message);
    }
}
```

In this code, `await` is used on the result of `Promise.all()` to cause the function to wait until either all of the promises have been fulfilled or one of them is rejected (in which case an error is thrown). The three promises are free to be fulfilled in parallel while the function waits. Here's an example of reading multiple files in Node.js:

```
import { readFile } from "node:fs/promises";

async function readFiles(filenames) {
    const fileContents = await Promise.all(
        filenames.map(filename => readFile(filename, "utf8"))
    );

    return fileContents.map(
        fileContent => JSON.parse(fileContent)
    );
}
```

```
readFiles([
    "file1.json",
    "file2.json"
]).then(data => {

    // process as necessary
    console.log(data);

}).catch(reason => {
    console.error(reason.message);
});
```

The `readFiles()` async function uses `await` with `Promise.all()` to wait for all of the files to be read. The file contents can then be parsed as JSON to return the data in the most appropriate format for processing.

> Of course, you can also use `await` with `Promise.allSettled()`, `Promise.any()`, `Promise.race()`, or any other function that returns a promise.

Using the `for-await-of` Loop

Another special syntax enabled inside async functions is the `for-await-of` loop, which allows you to retrieve values from an iterable or an async iterable. An *iterable* is an object with a `Symbol.iterator` method that returns an iterator; an *async iterable* is an object with a `Symbol.asyncIterator` method that returns an iterator whose values are always promises. The `for-await-of` loop calls `Promise.resolve()` on each value returned from an iterable and then waits for each promise to resolve before continuing to the next iteration of the loop.

The most often used iterables in JavaScript are arrays, and so you can use an array of promises with a `for-await-of` loop to process promises in sequence, as in this example:

```
const promise1 = Promise.resolve(1);
const promise2 = Promise.resolve(2);
const promise3 = Promise.resolve(3);
```

```
for await (const value of [promise1, promise2, promise3]) {
    console.log(value);
}
```

This example processes `promise1`, `promise2`, and `promise3` in that order. Even though these are settled promises, the `for-await-of` loop works on unsettled promises as well. And because the `for-await-of` loop always calls `Promise.resolve()` on any value retrieved from an iterable, you can use it directly on arrays, like this:

```
for await (const value of [1, 2, 3]) {
    console.log(value);
}
```

Even though there are no promises in the array in this example, the `for-await-of` loop will still work.

The most often used async iterables in Node.js are `ReadStream` objects. A `ReadStream` object is used to periodically read data from a source where all of the data may not be available. For network requests, reading large files, or event streams, `ReadStream` objects are a convenient way to work with such data. Here's an example:

```
import fs from "node:fs";

async function readCompleteTextStream(readable) {
    readable.setEncoding("utf8");

    let data = "";
    for await (const chunk of readable) {
        data += chunk;
    }

    return data;
}

const stream = fs.createReadStream("data.txt");
readCompleteTextStream(stream)
    .then(text => console.log(text));
```

The readCompleteTextStream() function accepts a ReadStream object called readable as a parameter. The first step to reading a text file is to set the encoding to "utf8" using the setEncoding() method. Then, a for-await-of loop iterates over the data read from readable. If the file is short, then there may only be one chunk of data; if the file is long, then there will likely be multiple chunks of data. Using the for-await-of loop allows you to not worry about the number of chunks being returned.

Similar to the await expression, a for-await-of loop throws an error if any of the promises returned from the async iterable are rejected. You can catch that error with a try-catch statement inside of the async function, such as:

```
import fs from "node:fs";

async function readCompleteTextStream(readable) {
    readable.setEncoding("utf8");

    try {
        let data = "";
        for await (const chunk of readable) {
            data += chunk;
        }
        return data;
    } catch (error) {
        console.error(error.message);
    }
}

const stream = fs.createReadStream("data.txt");
readCompleteTextStream(stream)
    .then(text => console.log(text));
```

In this example, the first rejected promise in the for-await-of loop causes an error to be thrown. The try-catch statement can then catch the error and log it to the console. Without the try-catch statement, a rejected promise in the for-await-of loop will be caught and returned as a rejected promise from the readCompleteTextStream() function.

Top-Level Await Expressions

You can also use `await` at the top level of a JavaScript module outside of an async function. Essentially, a JavaScript module acts as an async function wrapped around the entire module by default. This allows you to call promise-based functions directly, such as using the `import()` function:

```
// static import
import something from "./file.js";

// dynamic import
const filename = "./another-file.js";
const somethingElse = await import(filename);
```

Using top-level `await`, you can load modules dynamically alongside the statically loaded modules. (Dynamically loaded modules allow you to construct the module specifier dynamically, as well, which is not possible with static `import`.) This example uses both a static import and a dynamic import to illustrate the difference.

When the JavaScript engine encounters a top-level `await`, the JavaScript module execution is paused until the promise is settled. If the parent module of the paused module has static imports to process then those can continue even while the sibling module using top-level `await` is paused. The order in which the sibling modules are loaded cannot be guaranteed in this situation, but that order should not matter in most situations.

> Top-level `await` expressions cannot be used in JavaScript scripts. In order to use top-level `await`, you must load your JavaScript code using `import` or `<script type="module">`.

Summary

Async functions allow you to use promises without manually assigning fulfillment and rejection handlers. You can turn any function into an async function by adding the `async` keyword before the function definition.

The return value of an async function is always a promise. If you return a promise from the async function, then it is duplicated and returned to the call site; if you return a non-promise value, then the value is resolved to a promise and returned to the call site.

Errors thrown inside an async function are caught and returned as a rejected promise. Due to this behavior, you cannot catch errors originating in an async function using `try-catch`; instead, you need to assign a rejection handler to the returned promise.

Async functions enable two special types of syntax: the `await` expression and the `for-await-of` loop. The `await` expression is used to automatically assign fulfillment and rejection handlers to a promise such that the fulfillment value becomes the return value of the `await` expression and a rejection causes an error to be thrown. Similarly, the `for-await-of` loop operates on an async iterable and allows the use of promises instead of a loop. The `for-await-of` loop waits for each promise returned from the async iterable to fulfill before going on to the next promise. If a promise from the async iterable is rejected, then an error is thrown.

You can use top-level `await` expressions outside of async functions at the top level of JavaScript modules. This capability is not available in scripts.

5. Unhandled Rejection Tracking

In the first generation of promises, a rejected promise without a rejection handler would silently fail. Many considered this the biggest flaw in the specification as it was the only part of the JavaScript language that didn't make errors apparent. Later, JavaScript runtimes instituted console warnings to at least notify developers when unhandled rejections occurred, and some decided to throw errors. Eventually, unhandled rejection tracking was added into the JavaScript specification.

Detecting Unhandled Rejections

Determining whether a promise rejection was handled isn't straightforward due to the nature of promises. For instance, consider this example:

```
let rejected = Promise.reject(42);

// at this point, rejected is unhandled

setTimeout(() => {

    rejected.catch(value => {
        // now rejected has been handled
        console.log(value);
    });

}, 5000);
```

You can call then() or catch() at any point and have them work correctly regardless of whether the promise is settled or not, making it hard to know precisely when a promise is going to be handled. In this case, the promise is rejected immediately but isn't handled until later.

The JavaScript specification considers a promise to be handled if the promise's then() method has been called (which includes catch() and finally(), both of which call then() behind the scenes). It actually doesn't matter if you've attached a fulfillment handler, a rejection handler, or neither, so long as then() was called. Each call to then() creates a new promise which then becomes responsible for dealing with any fulfillment or rejection. Consider this example:

```
const promise1 = new Promise((resolve, reject) => {
    reject(43);
});

const promise2 = promise1.then(value => {
    console.log(value);
});
```

Here, promise1 is considered handled because then() is called and a fulfillment handler is attached. When promise1 is rejected, that rejection is passed on to promise2, which is not handled. A runtime would report the unhandled rejection from promise2 and disregard promise1. So, the runtime isn't really tracking all unhandled rejections, but rather, it's tracking whether the last promise in a chain has any handlers attached.

While the JavaScript specification does indicate how to track unhandled rejections, it doesn't specify what a runtime should do when an unhandled rejection occurs. Those details are left to the runtimes themselves as the appropriate reaction may be different depending on where the runtime is executed.

Web Browser Unhandled Rejection Tracking

Unhandled rejection tracking for web browsers is defined in the HTML specification. At the core of unhandled rejection tracking are two events that are emitted by the `globalThis` object:

- `unhandledrejection`: Emitted when a promise is rejected and no rejection handler is called within one turn of the event loop.
- `rejectionhandled`: Emitted when a promise is rejected and a rejection handler is called after one turn of the event loop.

These two events are designed to be used together to accurately detect unhandled promise rejections. Here's an example showing when each event is triggered:

```
const rejected = Promise.reject(new Error("Oops!"));

setTimeout(() => {

    // "rejectionhandled" triggered here
    rejected.catch(
        reason => console.error(reason.message)    // "Oops!"
    );

}, 500);

// "unhandledrejection" triggered at this point
```

In this code, `rejected` is a rejected promise that has no rejection handler attached initially. The `unhandledrejection` event is emitted once the script task has completed to let you know that a rejected promise exists without a rejection handler. The timer adds a rejection handler after a delay of 500 milliseconds, at which point the `rejectionhandled` event is emitted to let you know that a promise previously flagged as having an unhandled rejection has now been handled. That means you need to track the promises triggering these events in order to accurately detect problems.

Both `unhandledrejection` and `rejectionhandled` generate an `event` object containing the following properties:

- `type`: The name of the event (`"unhandledrejection"` or `"rejectionhandled"`)
- `promise`: The promise object that was rejected
- `reason`: The rejection value from the promise

With this information you can track which promises don't have rejection handlers, as in this example:

```
const rejected = Promise.reject(new Error("Oops!"));

setTimeout(() => {

    // "rejectionhandled" triggered here
    rejected.catch(
        reason => console.error(reason.message)    // "Oops!"
    );

}, 500);

globalThis.onunhandledrejection = event => {
    console.log(event.type);                       // "unhandledrejection"
    console.log(event.reason.message);             // "Oops!"
    console.log(rejected === event.promise);        // true
};

globalThis.onrejectionhandled = event => {
    console.log(event.type);                       // "rejectionhandled"
    console.log(event.reason.message);             // "Oops!"
    console.log(rejected === event.promise);        // true
};

// "unhandledrejection" triggered at this point
```

This code assigns both event handlers using the DOM Level 0 notation of `onunhandledrejection` and `onrejectionhandled`. (You can also use `addEventListener()` in both cases if you prefer.) Each event handler receives an event object containing information about the rejected promise. The `type`, `promise`, and `reason` properties are all available in both event handlers.

Even though this section focuses on unhandled rejection tracking in web browsers, Deno has decided to implement the HTML specification's unhandled rejection tracking as part of its web platform compatibility. Everything discussed in this section, therefore, also applies to Deno even when not explicitly mentioned.

> At the time of this writing, Deno has implemented `unhandledrejection` and `rejectionhandled` events for workers but not for the main thread. This issue is actively being worked on and should be resolved soon.

Reporting Unhandled Rejections in Web Browsers

While the `unhandledrejection` and `rejectionhandled` events are helpful in identifying potential problems, they are not useful for tracking problems in production without some addition functionality. You don't necessarily want to log every unhandled rejection because a rejection handler may be added later, so it makes sense to specify a timeframe within which you expect all promise rejections to be handled. For instance, you might want to log every rejection that hasn't been handled within a minute. To do so, you need to track promises that triggered `unhandledrejection` but did not trigger `rejectionhandled`. Here's one approach to doing that:

```
const possiblyUnhandledRejections = new Map();

// when a rejection is unhandled, add it to the map
globalThis.onunhandledrejection = event => {
    possiblyUnhandledRejections.set(event.promise, event.reason);
};

// when a rejection is handled, remove it from the map
globalThis.onrejectionhandled = event => {
    possiblyUnhandledRejections.delete(event.promise);
};

setInterval(() => {

    possiblyUnhandledRejections.forEach((reason, promise) => {

        console.error("Unhandled rejection");
```

```
        console.error(promise);
        console.error(reason.message ? reason.message : reason);

        // do something to handle these rejections
    });

    possiblyUnhandledRejections.clear();

}, 60000);
```

This is a simple unhandled rejection tracker. It uses a map to store promises and their rejection reasons. Each promise is a key, and the promise's reason is the associated value. Each time `unhandledrejection` is emitted, the promise and its rejection reason are added to the map. Each time `rejectionhandled` is emitted, the handled promise is removed from the map. As a result, `possiblyUnhandledRejections` grows and shrinks as events are emitted. The `setInterval()` call periodically checks the list of possible unhandled rejections and outputs the information to the console (in reality, you'll probably want to do something else to log or otherwise handle the rejection). A map is used in this example instead of a weak map because you need to inspect the map periodically to see which promises are present, and that's not possible with a weak map.

Preventing Console Warnings in Web Browsers

By default, browsers and Deno will output uncaught rejections to the console, and that doesn't change because you're listening for the `uncaughtrejection` event. You can prevent the console warning by calling `event.preventDefault()` inside the `onuncaughtrejection` event handler, as in this example:

```
globalThis.onunhandledrejection = event => {

    // prevents the console warning
    event.preventDefault();
};
```

This example prevents the console warning but doesn't affect the relationship with the `rejectionhandled` event, which will still be emitted if the promise that triggered `unhandledrejection` is later assigned a rejection handler.

Handling Unhandled Rejections in Web Browsers

Another quirk in the relationship between the `unhandledrejection` and `rejectionhandled` events is that you can prevent the `rejectionhandled` event from firing by adding a rejection handler inside of the `onunhandledrejection` event handler, like this:

```
globalThis.onunhandledrejection = ({ promise, reason }) => {
    promise.catch(() => {});      // handle the rejection
};

// this will never be called
globalThis.onrejectionhandled = ({ promise }) => {
    console.log(promise);
};
```

In this case, the `rejectionhandled` event isn't triggered because a rejection handler is added before it's time for that event. The browser assumes that you know the promise is now handled and so there is no reason to trigger the `rejectionhandled` event.

> A console warning will still be output even after handling a rejection inside of `onunhandledrejection` unless you also call `event.preventDefault()` inside of `onunhandledrejection`.

Node.js Unhandled Rejection Tracking

Node.js tracks unhandled promise rejections in a similar, but not the same, way as browsers. There are two events in Node.js, but these are emitted on the `process` object and have different capitalization than the browser events:

- `unhandledRejection`: Emitted when a promise is rejected and no rejection handler is called within one turn of the event loop.
- `rejectionHandled`: Emitted when a promise is rejected and a rejection handler is called after one turn of the event loop.

Also unlike the browser events, these events do not receive an `event` object. The `unhandledRejection` event handler is passed the rejection reason and the promise that was rejected as arguments. The following code shows `unhandledRejection` in action:

```
const rejected = Promise.reject(new Error("Oops!"));

process.on("unhandledRejection", (reason, promise) => {
    console.log(reason.message);           // "Oops!"
    console.log(rejected === promise);     // true
});
```

This example creates a rejected promise with an error object and listens for the `unhandledRejection` event. The event handler receives the error object as the first argument and the promise as the second.

The `rejectionHandled` event handler has only one argument, which is the promise that was rejected. For example:

```
const rejected = Promise.reject(new Error("Oops!"));

setTimeout(() => {

    // "rejectionhandled" triggered here
    rejected.catch(
        reason => console.error(reason.message) // "Oops!"
    );

}, 500);

process.on("rejectionHandled", promise => {
    console.log(rejected === promise);   // true
});
```

Here, the `rejectionHandled` event is emitted when the rejection handler is finally called. Note that, unlike in the browser, the reason for the rejection isn't passed into the `rejectionHandled` event handler.

By default, Node.js throws an error when an unhandled promise rejection occurs unless there is an event handler for unhandledRejection. You can change how Node.js handles uncaught promise rejections by using the --unhandled-rejection command-line option.

- --unhandled-rejection=throw (default) means that the unhandledRejection event is emitted. If there is no event handler specified for unhandledRejection, then the rejection reason is thrown as an error that can be caught by using an uncaughtException event handler. If no uncaughtException handler is specified, then the Node.js process exits with process.exitCode set to 1.
- --unhandled-rejection=strict means that the unhandledRejection event is not emitted. Instead, the rejection reason is thrown as that can be caught using an uncaughtException event handler. Any unhandledRejection handlers are not executed.
- --unhandled-rejection=warn means that the unhandledRejection event is emitted and a warning will always be output to the console regardless if any unhandledRejection handlers are defined. There is no change to the process exit code.
- --unhandled-rejection=warn-with-error-code acts the same as --unhandled-rejection=warn except that when the process exits it does so with process.exitCode set to 1 if no other exit code is specified.
- --unhandled-rejection=none completely ignores any unhandled promise rejections. There is no console output and the process continues executing JavaScript.

For production deployments, the --unhandled-rejection=strict is recommended as a promise rejection may leave the application in an unstable state in a manner that is similar to an uncaught error.

Reporting Unhandled Rejections in Node.js

To properly track potentially unhandled rejections, use the unhandledRejection and rejectionHandled events to keep a list of potentially unhandled rejections (similar to the web browser approach). Here is a Node.js-specific version of the simple rejection tracker described earlier in this chapter for web browsers:

```
const possiblyUnhandledRejections = new Map();

// when a rejection is unhandled, add it to the map
process.on("unhandledRejection", (reason, promise) => {
    possiblyUnhandledRejections.set(promise, reason);
});

process.on("rejectionHandled", promise => {
    possiblyUnhandledRejections.delete(promise);
});

setInterval(() => {

    possiblyUnhandledRejections.forEach((reason, promise) => {

        console.error("Unhandled rejection");
        console.error(promise);
        console.error(reason.message ? reason.message : reason);

        // do something to handle these rejections
    });

    possiblyUnhandledRejections.clear();

}, 60000);
```

The algorithm for this rejection tracker is the same as in the web browser example; it just uses the Node.js-specific functionality instead. Otherwise, `possiblyUnhandledRejections` grows and shrinks as events are called and `setInterval()` is used to periodically check the list of possible unhandled rejections and output the information to the console.

Summary

All JavaScript runtimes track unhandled promise rejections in some way. Web browsers and Deno implement the algorithm specified in the HTML specification while Node.js implements its own solution. Both solutions rely on two events: one that is emitted when an untracked promise rejection occurs and one that is emitted if a previously untracked promise rejection has a rejection handler added.

The `unhandledrejection` event is emitted on the `globalThis` object in web browsers and Deno whenever an unhandled rejection is detected. Event handlers for `unhandledrejection` receive an `event` object containing the type of event, the promise that was rejected, and the reason for the promise rejection. The `rejectionhandled` event is emitted when a previously untracked promise rejection has a rejection handler added. Event handlers for `rejectionhandled` also receive an `event` object that also contains the event type, the promise, and the rejection reason.

Node.js also uses two events, but they occur on the `process` object and have slightly different names: `unhandledRejection` and `rejectionHandled`. Event handlers for `unhandledRejection` receive the rejection reason and the promise as arguments; event handlers for `rejectionHandled` receive just the promise.

Both approaches allow you to implement unhandled rejection reporting for your application by listening for both events and tracking the promises they provide in a separate location. You can then periodically check the list of promises to report them into your logging or reporting system.

Final Thoughts

When promises were added into the JavaScript language in 2015, they were a source of controversy and the topic of many thinkpieces opining whether this was the right way to address the asynchronous future of JavaScript. After several years, the dust has settled and promises have won many over, especially with the introduction of async functions in 2017. All new asynchronous JavaScript APIs are built to make use of promises, so understanding how to work with promises is an important part of any JavaScript-focused job.

I hope you've enjoyed this exploration of JavaScript promises.

Download the Extras

You can download companion materials for this book from https://bit.ly/promises-extras. The extras include:

1. A promises cheat sheet
2. All of the examples from the book
3. Frequently asked questions about promises

Support the Author

It takes a lot of time and effort to create a book like this. If you'd like to support my work, and get free copies of future e-books, please visit https://bit.ly/support-nzakas.

Help and Support

If you have any questions or comments about this book, please email books@humanwhocodes.com. Be sure to mention the title of this book in the subject line.

Follow the Author

You can follow Nicholas C. Zakas on the following sites:

- **Blog:** humanwhocodes.com
- **Twitter:** @slicknet, @humanwhocodes
- **GitHub:** @nzakas, @humanwhocodes
- **Instagram:** @nzakas, @humanwhocodes

Reach out and say hi!

CPSIA information can be obtained
at www.ICGtesting.com
Printed in the USA
LVHW051530020622
720196LV00007B/525